Weather Every Day

by Katherine Scraper

Table of Contents

blizzard

clouds

flood

hurricane

tornado

wind

What Is Weather?

We see, hear, and feel weather every day. The temperature is part of weather. The **wind** is part of weather. Precipitation is part of weather, too.

▲ The temperature is hot today.

▲ The girl can feel the wind.

| rain | snow | sleet | hail |

▲ We have four types of precipitation.

The temperature, wind, and precipitation work together. Temperature, wind, and precipitation make different types of weather. Weather can change quickly. The weather can also change slowly.

January	February	March
30° Fahrenheit −1° Celsius	36° Fahrenheit 2° Celsius	46° Fahrenheit 8° Celsius
April	**May**	**June**
55° Fahrenheit 13° Celsius	65° Fahrenheit 18° Celsius	76° Fahrenheit 24° Celsius
July	**August**	**September**
81° Fahrenheit 27° Celsius	80° Fahrenheit 26° Celsius	71° Fahrenheit 22° Celsius
October	**November**	**December**
59° Fahrenheit 15° Celsius	44° Fahrenheit 7° Celsius	34° Fahrenheit 1° Celsius

▲ Temperature can change slowly.

▲ Rain can come quickly.

What Is Extreme Weather?

The weather can be extreme sometimes. A **blizzard** is a storm. A blizzard brings a large amount of snow. The wind is very strong in a blizzard. A blizzard has cold temperatures, too. People must stay inside to be safe.

▲ The wind blows snow in a blizzard.

A **tornado** has very strong winds that spin quickly. Tornadoes move over the ground. People must find a place to be safe.

▲ A tornado can cause damage.

Some extreme weather brings **floods**.
A large amount of rain makes rivers rise.
Soon, the water moves over the land.
Sometimes, people must leave their homes
to be safe.

▲ A flood can get into people's homes.

A **hurricane** is a huge storm. The storm starts over the ocean. A hurricane brings strong winds and rain. Waves from the ocean bring floods. People must find a place to be safe.

▲ A hurricane can cause damage.

How Do We Measure Weather?

We observe, or see, weather every day. We see different types of **clouds**.

▲ Different types of clouds bring different types of weather.

We measure weather, too.
A thermometer measures temperature.
A weather vane measures the direction
of the wind. A rain gauge measures
how much precipitation falls.

▲ thermometer   ▲ weather vane   ▲ rain gauge

The things we observe and measure give us data. People record data about weather every day.

	Clouds	Wind Direction	Temperature	Rainfall
Sunday		from southeast to northwest	65° Fahrenheit 18° Celsius	0 inches 0 centimeters
Monday				
Tuesday				
Wednesday				
Thursday				
Friday				
Saturday				

▲ Pictures can be data. Numbers can be data, too.

We use the data to learn about weather.
People gather data all over the world.

July 10, 2007
Buenos
Aires

▲ Buenos Aires had snow on July 10, 2007.
Buenos Aires did not have snow for 89 years!

How Do We Predict Weather?

We use data to predict weather, too. We find out what type of weather to expect.

▲ This woman uses data to predict the weather.

Knowing what to expect helps people make plans. People can be safe if extreme weather is coming.

▲ The weather is nice.
This family is having a picnic.

▲ The weather is extreme.
This family is staying home.

We have weather every day. What type of weather do you like best?